WONDERS
OF THE WORLD

Crop
Circles

Other books in the Wonders of the World series include:

WONDERS
OF THE WORLD

Crop Circles

Jan Burns

KIDHAVEN PRESS

An imprint of Thomson Gale, a part of The Thomson Corporation

THOMSON

————✦————™

GALE

Detroit • New York • San Francisco • San Diego • New Haven, Conn.
Waterville, Maine • London • Munich

© 2006 Thomson Gale, a part of The Thomson Corporation.

Thomson and Star Logo are trademarks and Gale and KidHaven Press are registered trademarks used herin under license.

For more information, contact
KidHaven Press
27500 Drake Rd.
Farmington Hills, MI 48331-3535
Or you can visit our Internet site at http://www.gale.com

LIBRARY OF CONGRESS CATALOGING-IN-PUBLICATION DATA

Burns, Jan
  Crop circles / by Jan Burns.
    p. cm. — (Wonders of the world)
  Includes bibliographical references and index.
  Contents: What are crop circles?—Appearance of complex crop circle formations—How crop circles are formed—Learning more about crop circles.
  ISBN 0-7377-3063-3 (hardcover : alk. paper)
  1. Crop circles—Juvenile literature. I. Title. II. Wonders of the world (KidHaven Press)
  AG243.B788 2005
  001.94—dc22

                                                            2005007812

Printed in the United States of America

CONTENTS

What Are Crop Circles?

Some things in the world remain mysterious. These things are called **phenomena**. They puzzle and fascinate people. Crop circles are one of these mysterious things. They are large, perfect circles cut into crop fields. The crop stalks inside the circles are bent over to the ground in a spiral pattern. Curiously, they do not seem to be made by humans. There are no footprints, paths, or clues of any kind as to who created them.

Most crop circles have appeared in southern England. Each appearance has created widespread interest. People are curious about them and want to know who created them and why.

Early Crop Circles

Researcher Lucy Pringle discovered a surprising fact about crop circles: They are not a new phenomenon.

Many elderly inhabitants of southern England have stated that they remember playing in crop circles when they were children in the 1930s and 1940s. One woman said that the adults took no notice of the appearance of the crop circles and did not bother to take pictures of them or contact any newspapers about them.

First Documented Crop Circle

Seeing a crop circle form is extremely rare. Only a few dozen people have seen it happen. Most circles are discovered after they have been formed. The first documented

A young girl runs across a large crop circle in southern England.

case of a person witnessing the formation of a crop circle occurred in Warminster, England, on August 15, 1972. Arthur Shuttlewood was out walking with a friend when, he claimed, something strange started to happen. Grain in a field before him flattened out like a fan. A circle formed in less than a minute. He heard a high-pitched tone. Although he was momentarily stunned, he and his companion started talking about what they had seen. Shuttlewood then inspected the area and discovered two more circles. He had no idea how they were created.

Tourist Discovers Crop Circles

Early one morning in 1980, a tourist was walking on a trail above a valley in Wiltshire, England, when he was startled to see three large circles cut into the field below. They were not there the day before. The tourist called a local newspaper, the *Wiltshire Times*, to report the circles.

Three identical circles, each about 60 feet (20m) in diameter, were cut into a field of oats. The outlines of the circles were clearly cut, so the shapes were easily recognizable. The plant stalks in the middle were flattened into a spiral pattern. They looked like swirls. Surprisingly, whatever or whoever had made the circles had not damaged the flattened stalks; they were only pushed down. This was odd, because crop stalks are usually damaged if they are flattened in any way.

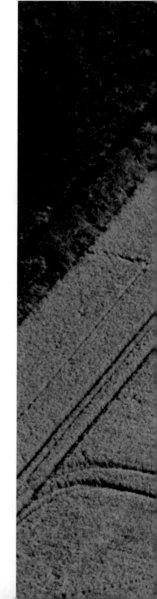

There were no footprints, paths, or clues of any kind as to who had created the circles. There were no ruts or tire tracks inside the circles, so it was unlikely that any machinery was used to create them. The swirled patterns in the middle seemed too perfectly formed to have

These crop circles in a wheat field in Oxfordshire, England, appeared in a group.

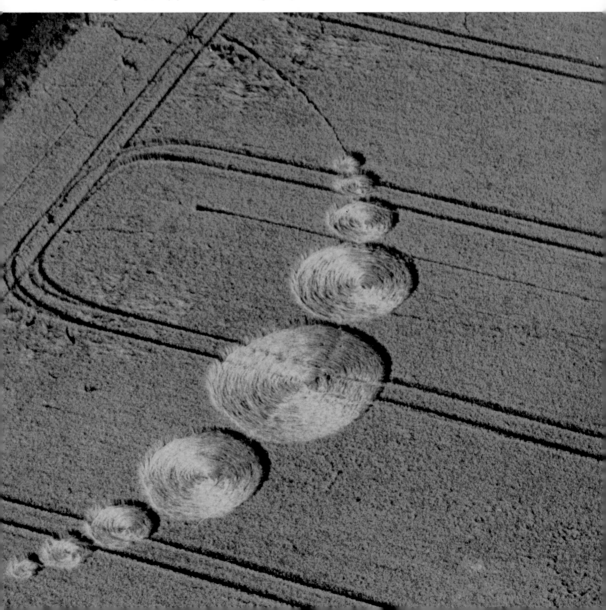

Although crop stalks in the middle of the circles are flattened, the stalks are not damaged or broken.

been created by hand. Most people had never seen anything like them before.

The field's owner was interviewed for the article. He said that he had never seen marks or patterns like those found inside the crop circles. He said he had seen plenty of wind and rain damage, and the marks did not look like either of them.

Ian Mrzyglod, a **UFO** researcher, examined the circles. He saw that the crop stalks in the middle of the circles were not broken. They were bent at the root. They looked like they had been swept down gently.

Terence Meaden, an atmospheric physicist and a founding member of the Tornado and Storm Research Organization for Britain, noted that it was hot and windless the day the circles had appeared. Whirlwinds sometimes rise up from the ground during that kind of weather. He suggested that the circles might have been formed by stationary whirlwinds. However, he stated, whirlwinds tend to move randomly. He had never heard of them making a circle. If a whirlwind had created a circle, the circle would be an **anomaly**, not the usual type of shape a whirlwind tended to make.

Before these circles appeared, no **in-depth** study of crop circles had ever been done. Meaden and others who were interested in the phenomenon started to gather data about the circles and to develop theories about their formation.

Hampshire, England, Crop Circles

On August 19, 1981, a friend asked Pat Delgado to see if he could figure out what might have caused some circles at Cheesefoot Head, in Hampshire, in southern England. Delgado was a retired electromechanical engineer. He had an inquisitive mind and the time to research things that intrigued him.

He traveled to the site and viewed the circles. There was one large circle, about 60 feet (20m) in diameter, with two smaller circles, each about 25 feet (8m) in diameter, on either side of it. The circles were in a straight line. Again, there were no footprints or other signs of entry into the field.

Delgado later stated that the circles had a profound effect on him. As he gazed at them, he considered all the possible ways they could have been created. He thought other people would also be interested in seeing them. He contacted several national newspapers, as well as the British Broadcasting Corporation (BBC), to report what he had seen.

Meaden was asked if he thought these circles also could have been created by stationary whirlwinds. He said that it was pos-

The intricate designs of crop circles, like these in England (left) and California (above), draw thousands of curious sightseers.

sible, because the field in question was on a concave, punch-bowl slope. This might have caused an atmospheric disturbance to jump up and down and form the circles.

Circles Cause Excitement

Thousands of people became interested in the crop circles that appeared in southern England. They eagerly

This star-shaped formation in an English field shows just how complex crop circle designs can be.

read about the circles in the newspapers, and many drove out to see new ones as soon as they appeared.

Each new crop circle sparked more questions. Were the crop circles hoaxes? Were they caused by UFOs, whirlwinds, or some unknown forces?

Appearance of Complex Crop Circle Formations

The crop circle phenomenon became even more mysterious in the 1990s. Crop circle designs began to change. Before they had been simple circles. In the 1990s, crop circle formations became more complex. They contained squares, triangles, rectangles, and many other shapes. This change was puzzling. Researchers tried to discover their meaning and their origin.

Complicated Patterns

One of the first of these complex formations appeared on July 12, 1990, near Alton Barnes, in southern England. Early that morning a loud rumbling noise had been heard throughout the village. Dogs started barking and refused to stop. When farmer Tim Carson went out to check his fields, he found a 185-yard- long formation (168m).

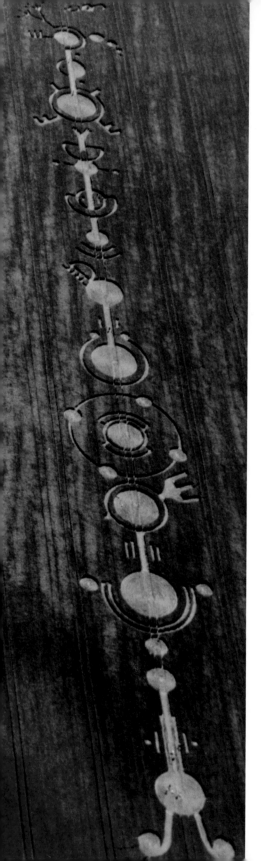

Delgado later said that the pattern of the crop circle was so complicated that an exact description of it would fill several pages. It was made up of squares, rectangles, and **tridents**, and had narrow spiral twists in the middle.

The formation also seemed to have a strange type of energy. A number of cars would not start that morning. Their owners found that their car batteries were mysteriously dead. One villager claimed that he had tried to walk into the formation at daybreak, but had been **repelled** by an invisible energy field. When a camera crew came in later, their recording equipment failed whenever they brought it inside the formation.

Pictures of the formation were printed in newspapers around the world. Thousands of people rushed to see it. Visitors came from as far away as Japan.

The following year, in 1991, a wide and sometimes puzzling vari-

More complicated crop-circle patterns, such as this one in Alton Barnes, England, began to appear in the 1990s.

ety of crop circles appeared. Of the 200 to 300 recorded circles, 60 were complex formations. Symbols started to appear in some of them. Crop circle researchers and others tried to **decipher** these symbols. They thought that an advanced civilization might be trying to use symbols to send messages.

In August 1991 a woman had a strange encounter with a UFO that seemed related to the circles. The woman was driving at 1:15 A.M. in the Cambridgeshire area when she realized her car was being followed by a silver-blue light sphere. After following her car closely for a while, the sphere disappeared. The next morning, a pilot flying to work discovered a formation in the area. It had not been there the day before.

Geometric Precision

The formation was a representation of what is known in mathematics as a Mandelbrot Set. It is a **geometric** figure named for Benoit Mandelbrot, the French mathematician who discovered it. It involves a mathematical figure of **fractal geometry**. A fractal is a mathematical pattern made by repeating the same pattern again and again, but moving, rotating, and changing its size each time. Geometry is a branch of mathematics that deals with shapes.

A local farm-crop specialist and biologist named Wombwell examined the formation. He said that it was incredibly precise. Each circle was perfect. Every stalk had been flattened 0.25 inch (6.4mm) above the soil. There were no footprints and no sign that machinery had been used.

Formed near Cambridge, England, in 1991, this design, known as a Mandelbrot Set, is thought by some to have been made by a UFO.

Britain's *New Science* magazine wrote that it would be impossible to construct this figure without a computer and a lot of time. Newspapers printed pictures of it with stories guessing how it was created. Ultimately, no one had any idea of how it could have been done.

The crop circles continued until 1993. Many had a type of dumbbell design. Researchers started to compare crop circles to similar types of symbols used in different cultures. For example, the dumbbell design was similar to one in Native American folklore. This symbol has two circles united by a straight line. This symbolizes communication between spirit and flesh, or Heaven and Earth. Researchers wondered if the makers of the symbols could be using similar symbolism.

Many more crop circles appeared every year. Some farmers even started to charge visitors a fee to enter their fields to see the formations.

Dumbell-shaped crop circles use a symbol similar to one used in many Native American cultures.

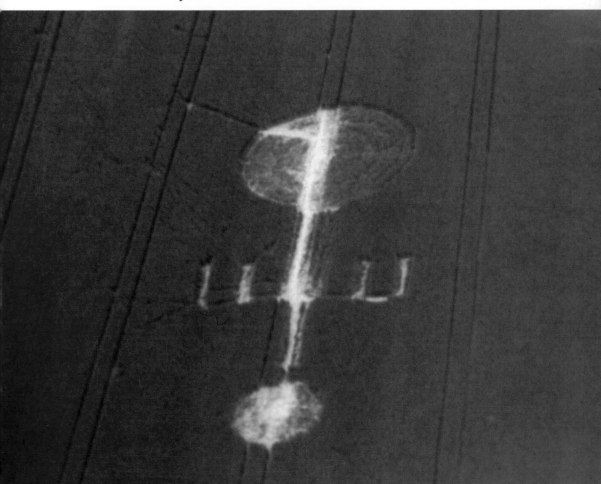

Crop Circle Formation Appears Mysteriously Near Stonehenge

Some crop circles received a lot of attention. One appeared near Stonehenge, the ancient stone monument formed about 2800 to 1500 B.C. A superhighway runs along one side of Stonehenge, while farmland lies beyond that. On July 7, 1996, a gigantic crop circle appeared on the farmland between 5:30 and 6:00 P.M. The sprawling formation was more than 330 yards (300m)

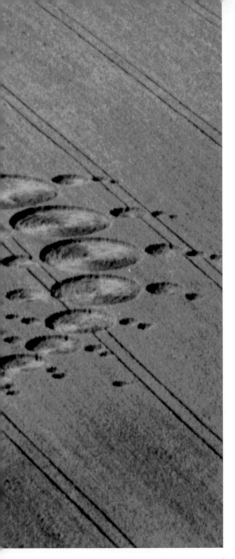

Called a Julia Set, this formation near the ancient stone monument of Stonehenge was formed in 1996 in just 30 minutes.

long and 163.6 yards (152m) wide. It twisted into a spiral of 149 circles that varied in size from 1 foot (0.3m) to 50 feet (15.2m) in diameter. It was a representation of a computer-modeled fractal pattern named the Julia Set.

Although most crop circles appear between midnight and 6:00 A.M., the Julia Set appeared in the daytime. A Stonehenge security guard inspected the surrounding area with binoculars at 5:00 P.M. that day. Then a pilot flew over the field at 5:30 P.M., and the formation was not there. It was only when the pilot made a return pass over the field thirty minutes later that he discovered the Julia Set.

At first the owner of the field was convinced that the crop circle was made by **vandals**. From the ground it was difficult to see the complex design. When he saw aerial photos of it, however, he changed his mind. Soon afterward he put up a sign that said, "See Europe's Best Crop Circle." He asked for a donation to enter the field. More than 10,000 people visited the field over the next three weeks.

As crop circle research became more common, the study of the phenomenon became known as cereology, after Ceres, the Roman goddess of agriculture and fertility. Crop circle researchers are called cereologists.

Crop Circles Spread

Crop circles also started to appear in other countries. More than 10,000 circles have been found in more than 26 countries, including Russia, South Africa, China, France,

Crop circles have been found in more than 26 countries, including Switzerland, where this one appeared.

India, the United States, Canada, Australia, Japan, and others.

Southern England, however, remained the center of the crop circle activity. With newspapers reporting the stories, and farmers offering tours, crop circles had gripped the public's imagination.

How Crop Circles Are Formed

Crop circles appear mysteriously. They are discovered only after they have been constructed. Many theories, or ideas, have emerged concerning how crop circles are made.

UFO Landing Sites?

After pictures of crop circles appeared in newspapers and on television, some people believed that they could be UFO landing sites. One reason is that mysterious lights are often seen in the sky right before crop circles appear.

One such UFO sighting occurred on June 28, 1989, in southwestern England. An eyewitness saw a ball of

This computer illustration shows a UFO leaving a crop circle behind as it takes off from a wheat field.

light 30 to 40 feet (10 to 13m) in diameter. It came down over a field and lowered itself over the crop. The eye-witness reported that the underside of the sphere flattened out and then disappeared. A crop circle was found in the field in that spot the following day.

There are some connections, or similarities, between UFO sightings and crop circles. In both, animals in the area often become restless and disturbed. Cattle have broken through their fencing, and dogs run around barking as if looking for a prowler or possibly sensing danger. Sheep move as far away as possible from a particular field before a formation appears there.

UFO believers mention other phenomena that appear with crop circles. Compasses spin out of control, and electrical equipment fails within crop circles.

Others point out that there is no scientific proof that an alien life-form is responsible for any of the crop circles. They believe that if the circles were true landing spots for UFOs, that the middle of the crop circles would be damaged and would not have the swirled patterns. They also suggest that some people prefer the exciting idea of the presence of an alien life-form rather than a more scientific explanation for the crop circle phenomenon.

Hoaxes?

Many more people believe the circles are elaborate hoaxes. They point to a grouping of five crop circles, known as a quintuplet, that was discovered in Bratton, England, in 1983. Soon afterward, a second crop circle

This crop circle in England is a hoax. Many people
believe all crop circles are fakes.

quintuplet appeared nearby. Bob Rickard, the editor of
a magazine that investigates mysterious happenings, realized that the second crop circle formation did not look
like the first quintuplet. The edges of these circles were
roughly cut, not precise, like the earlier ones. Also, footprints were found. There were no prints in or around
the first quintuplet. He suggested that the second quintuplet was a fake.

This formation of one large crop circle surrounded by four smaller circles is known as a quintuplet.

Rickard was right. A local farmer and his son had entered the field on stilts and created the circles. They had been hired by a local newspaper, the *Daily Mirror,* to set up the hoax to trick a competing newspaper, the *Daily Express,* into reporting the circles as authentic.

The farmers eventually admitted that they had created the circles. They said they measured the circles with a pole and rope and flattened the crops down with a heavy chain.

With the right equipment and enough time and experience, some hoaxers can create authentic-looking crop circles. They do it for money, to compete with other crop circle hoaxers, because of a dare, or simply to get attention.

On September 9, 1991, Englishmen Doug Bower and Dave Chorley announced that they had created all the crop circles themselves, beginning in 1978. They claimed that they had made the circles with 4-foot long wooden planks (12m) tied beneath their feet. As they walked, the planks pushed down strips of crops.

They said they had made the crop circles for fun. Each year they made the designs in the circles more complex to confuse crop circle researchers. Bower and Chorley decided to go public with their admission because

Some people believe that humans are incapable of creating the intricate designs of some crop circles.

they were now in their sixties. They were getting too old to make the circles anymore.

Many people did not believe that the men were capable of making the complex crop designs themselves. They did not sound believable in interviews, because they kept changing their stories about how they had created them. No one could completely disprove their claims, however.

The Plasma-Vortex Theory

Bower and Chorley may have created some crop circles, but few believed they had made them all. People looking for a more scientific explanation found physicist Terence Meaden's ideas more believable.

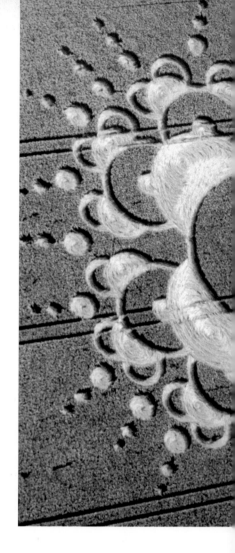

By 1990, Meaden had expanded on his earlier theory that whirlwinds and **eddies** could create crop circles. Ordinary whirlwinds, such as waterspouts and dust devils, suck things upward. They could not cause crop circles because the crops in the circles lay flat. There has to be a downward momentum on the crop stalks to make them do that. Meaden suggested that a unique kind of whirlwind could collapse in a descending burst of violent wind. This kind of whirlwind would produce a downward momentum that would push the crops flat.

Whirlwinds and eddies could never create complex formations like this one, in which one side perfectly mirrors the other.

This collapsing wind form, or **vortex**, is surrounded at times by a ring of electrically charged air, called **plasma**. It would have the ability to stay in the air for a few minutes before descending to the ground. It could quickly cut simple crop circles out of fields. It could also travel across a field, touching the ground, rising, and then touching down on the ground again. In this way it could produce a number of crop circles of differing sizes. Meaden felt that the low-lying hills of southern England supplied the perfect weather conditions to form this particular kind of whirlwind.

There were two significant facts about the theory that helped give it credibility. The electric currents and magnetic fields manufactured by rotating plasma can create light as well as a humming sound. Eyewitnesses who saw crop circles form have mentioned these two things. Also, plasmas can be luminous, which could explain why many people have reported seeing lights in the sky right before a crop circle appeared. Research is continuing on this theory.

What Forces Are at Work?

While the plasma-vortex theory seems to be a possible explanation for the simple crop circles, most researchers do not think a plasma vortex could create a complex crop circle. This has prompted thousands to question if the force that creates crop circles is simply too advanced for people to currently understand.

Some researchers claim that with time and more experiments they will be able to find an answer to the crop circle phenomenon. Other researchers believe that the unexplained force is controlled by extraterrestrials of advanced intelligence.

Learning More About Crop Circles

Crop circles continue to appear around the world. Each new formation contributes to the overall knowledge of the phenomenon. After years of data collection and on-site research, researchers have been able to establish some patterns.

To get their information, researchers interview the farmers who own the fields in which the crop circles form, and any other available witnesses. They photograph the formations from the air and **close-up** to get different visual perspectives of the crop circles. They also measure the circles, record the type of swirl pattern they have, and note any unique characteristics.

Researchers have found that most crop circles appear at the beginning of April each year and continue to form until **harvesttime**, which is usually in September. At the start

of the season, the designs are usually relatively simple. As the season progresses, the designs become more complex.

Most crop circles form close to a water source, such as a spring, pond, reservoir, or underground tank. Many crop circles also appear over areas where the **groundwater** is close to the surface. This has led some researchers to believe that the placement of crop circles might in some way be influenced by the subsurface water levels.

Magnetism also seems to have some involvement in crop circles. Pocketknives, watches, and bicycles have become magnetized when brought into crop circles. Another oddity occurred when a Japanese researcher discovered a battery pack, which should have had fourteen hours of available power, drained when it was placed on the floor of a new crop circle. Researchers are trying to get more specific answers to what exact role magnetism plays in crop circles.

After the original single circles appeared, the number of crop circles increased dramatically. Most researchers believe that nine out of ten, or 90 percent, of the crop circles formed after that time were hoaxes of one kind or another. No answer, however, can yet completely explain the existence of the remaining 10 percent of the circles.

Paranormal Explanation for Crop Circles?

To get that explanation, some researchers have looked at the past and have come up with a possible **paranormal** explanation for crop circles. Ninety percent of all crop circles have appeared in southern England. This area has been called an enchanted landscape, because it is particularly rich in ancient sites that are thousands of years old. These include Stonehenge and Silbury Hill, a large grassy mound located in Wiltshire. Formed in approximately 2500 B.C., it is believed to be the largest human-made prehistoric mound in Europe. Strange lights and other phenomena have often been reported near both sites. Because many crop circles have appeared near these ancient sites, as well as others, some crop circle researchers believe there is a link between crop circles and ancient sites.

This theory claims that ancient humans built sites at particular locations because these places were close to **ley lines**. These lines are believed to be a network of paths by which prehistoric peoples journeyed about Britain. They have also been called energy paths on Earth's surface. Ancient peoples held rituals and ceremonies at these sites, which were close to the ley lines.

Strange Energy

Crop circles have been shown to possess strange energetic properties. **Magnetic fields** that are stronger than Earth's magnetic field have been detected in them. Some researchers who believe the circles are created by an alien lifeform have questioned if the crop circles and ancient sites together act as beacons for incoming extraterrestrials.

In 2002 the movie *Signs* featured crop circles. In the movie it was suggested that extraterrestrials created crop circles as a sort of visual landmark, to help them navigate.

Some people believe a strong connection exists between ancient sites, such as Silbury Hill in southern England (pictured), and crop circles.

What Is the Attraction of the Crop Circles?

Some people who have walked inside a crop circle, or who have even stood close to one, have reported feeling nausea, a headache, or overly tired. Oddly, other people have reported pleasant feelings and mental clarity after walking into or standing close to a circle. Some people have even reported feeling joyful.

Earth Energy Theory

Others believe that crop circles are somehow created by Earth itself. They think it is trying to communicate a message to stop pollution and habitat destruction, and point to some of the crop circle formations as evidence of this. For example, some circles show a representation of dolphins, which are threatened by pollution. Another formation showed Earth with tears falling from it. Some ecologists see this as a warning of the dangers of the reduction of the rain forests and global warming, among other things.

Crop circles are objects of beauty, full of precision and mysterious details. Researchers point to their symbols, and say that symbolic writing is universal and more readable than any other type of writing.

Just as we are trying to communicate with other beings through this, maybe others are trying to communicate with us through the crop circles. When National Aeronautics and Space Administration (NASA) experts devel-

This crop circle featuring a very complex design appeared in a wheat field near Stonehenge in 1996.

oped the first interstellar message from mankind, it, too, contained geometric symbols, as well as the structure of the solar system, human figures, and mathematical, physical, and chemical formulas. This message, engraved on a golden plaque, has been traveling since the 1970s aboard the Pioneer 10 space probe.

Although many theories try to explain the mystery of crop circles, no one knows for sure how these strange formations are created.

More Research Is Needed

People are still fascinated and puzzled by crop circles. Each time a possible solution to their puzzle arises, another facet or another fact of their existence surfaces, leading to the need for further study.

More research is needed before an answer to the mystery of crop circles is found. Future developments in research and technology will probably enable scientists to learn the answer someday.

Glossary

anomaly: Anything that does not follow the usual rule or pattern; abnormal.

close-up: A picture taken with a camera so that the subject appears very close to the viewer.

decipher: To translate a message that is in code into ordinary language.

eddies: Small currents of air, water, etc. moving in circles against the main current.

fractal geometry: Mathematical pattern made by repeating the same simple pattern again and again, but moving, rotating, and changing its size each time.

geometric: Formed of straight lines, triangles, circles, and other shapes.

groundwater: The water beneath the surface of the ground.

harvesttime: The time of year when farm crops are ready to be harvested.

in-depth: Carefully worked out in detail.

ley lines: Lines that are believed to be a network of paths by which prehistoric people journeyed about Britain. They have also been called energy paths on Earth's surface.

magnetic fields: Areas around a magnet where its magnetic effect can be felt.

magnetism: The power that a magnet has.

paranormal: Anything that cannot be explained by scientific investigation.

phenomena: Remarkable or unexplained happenings.

plasma: Air that has become electrically charged.

repelled: Driven or forced back.

tridents: Spears with three prongs.

UFO: An Unidentified Flying Object, believed by some to come from outer space.

vandals: People who destroy or damage things on purpose.

vortex: Rotating mass of air or water.

For Further Exploration

Books

Pat Delgado and Pat Andrews, *Circular Evidence.* Grand Rapids, MI: Phanes, 1989. This book is written by two leading crop circle researchers. Their theories, some of their notes, and many beautiful crop circle pictures are included.

Chris Oxlade, *The Mystery of Crop Circles.* Des Plaines, IL: Heinemann, 1999. This book examines crop circles and theories about how they are formed.

Jim Schnabel, *Round in Circles.* Amherst, NY: Prometheus Books, 1994. This book offers interesting behind-the-scenes information about crop circles and crop circle researchers.

Freddy Silva, *Secrets in the Fields.* Charlottesville, VA: Hampton Roads, 2002. Freddy Silva has researched crop circles for years. This book offers an in-depth look at crop circles.

Colin Wilson and Damon Wilson, *The Mammoth Encyclopedia of the Unsolved.* New York: Carroll & Graf, 2000. This presents a good general overview of crop circles.

Web Sites

www.cropcircleinfo.com. This site offers an interesting and informative look at Colin Andrews's crop circle research. He was one of the first crop circle researchers.

www.cropcirclequest.com. This site has links to articles about crop circles, the Canadian crop circle research network, England's crop circle network, and top ongoing scientific investigations.

Index

Picture Credits

About the Author

Jan Burns has written many articles for newspapers and magazines. She holds a bachelor's degree in sociology from the University of California at Berkeley. She lives close to Houston, Texas, with her husband, Don, and sons, David and Matt.